Afroł ... n

by

CONTENTS

Second Edition
Copyright © MCMXCII by Alfred Publishing Co., Inc

All rights reserved.   Printed in USA.
ISBN 0-88284-151-3
Photo by Martin Cohen, courtesy of LP Music Group

FOREWORD

This is designed for band leaders, arrangers, percussionists and music educators needing a quick and easy reference for both correct rhythms and proper instruments to produce the Latin and Afro influence in today's exciting new music. Influences are far-reaching: from Jazz, to Pop, Concert Hall to Football Field, Vocal and Instrumental alike.

BAND LEADERS can use this book as a list for the correct instruments to use in order of importance should they wish to augment or transform a combo into a Latin-Afro rhythm section. Dancers relate quickly to this augmented rhythm section sound as a fresh departure from the usual melodic and harmonic sounds.

ARRANGERS can quickly and succinctly see the needed instrumentation and rhythms for an authentic dance rhythm effect. To achieve the ideal rhythmic background, the professional arranger cleverly combines the instrument-plus-rhythm-plus an innovative twist to best fit the musical setting.

PERCUSSIONISTS will find the collections of rhythms, instruments, and playing techniques as an ideal and practical percussion ensemble experience. Although the rhythm instruments are humble, the drum family will need considerable practice for suitable authenticity. Also, to really "swing", the pulse should be solid, rhythms clean, and balance suitable for all instruments to be clearly heard. All of the dance forms are self contained and could be used successfully behind soloists.

MUSIC EDUCATORS, BAND, ORCHESTRA AND JAZZ ENSEMBLE CONDUCTORS may consult this HANDY GUIDE to cleverly augment any arrangement successfully with both the correct rhythms and required instrument to remain in good taste with the musical style of the composition.

VOCAL CONDUCTORS will find this book an outstanding source for enhancing Latin, Jazz and Rock arrangements with extra Latin and Afro instruments.

CLASSROOM MUSIC TEACHERS in general music will find it an invaluable source of rhythms and instruments from which to teach all ages. Each rhythm can be demonstrated and techniques discussed as the class participates by combining the instruments into a colorful percussion ensemble. The varied dances could be performed with appropriate records, tapes or piano as the dance forms are explored and explained.

TIPS FOR GUIDE USE

- Timbales may be omitted when drum set is used.
- Rhythm section accessory instruments are most essential for basic dance rhythm flavor.
- Instruments are listed for each dance in order of importance. With a shortage of players, try to include at least one instrument from the drum family even if it is necessary to eliminate a less important accessory.
- If authentic instruments are difficult to acquire, substitute instruments are suggested.
- Drum set can substitute for the drum family (bongos, conga and timbales), freeing players to perform on the rhythm accessories.
- Remember basic playing techniques and notational explanations for instruments are available at the beginning of the book.
- A jazz-style Latin or Afro rhythm requires a different interpretation. The straight eighths (♫♫♫♫) are actually played ♪♪♪♪♪ and a conga drum which plays ♩♫♩ ♫ will actually play ♩♪♪♩ ♪♪ to produce a more flowing "swing" feel.
- Consult the *Arranger's Section* for Afro-Latin scoring suggestions.
- A *Glossary* can be found at the end of the book.
- The drum set has been added to all dance forms as an augmentation. Although not an authentic part of an Afro-Latin instrumentation, it adds another creative dimension to the percussion section sound.

Drum set is notated in the following manner:

	RIDE CYMBAL
	HIGH PITCHED TOM
	SNARE DRUM
	LOW PITCHED TOM
	HI-HAT
	BASS DRUM

(snares off unless indicated)

Note: *"Drum-Set Club Date Dictionary"* by Sandy Feldstein includes many of the Latin, Afro, Rock and Jazz rhythms contained in this book. Publisher: Alfred Publishing Co., Inc.

INSTRUMENTS USED FOR LATIN-AMERICAN DANCES IN FOUR

The basic techniques below are contained in the Rhumba.

CLAVES

BASIC "CINQUILLO" RHYTHM

Remember to cup your left hand when holding the clave. Strike with right hand clave while holding gently.

COWBELL

Strike the cowbell with a stick near the closed end (x) and open end (o). The open end of the bell faces away from the player.

MARACAS

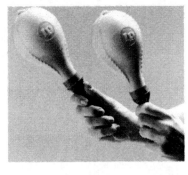

Develop clear clicks between hands; wrist action will produce this.

L R L R L R L R   L R L R L R L R

4

GUIRO

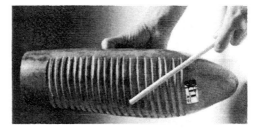

Legato notes should be played with a long scrape while staccato notes a short scrape. Tone is altered with scrape speed and pressure, stick size and if tip or center of scraper contacts the ridges.

D = Down stroke
U = Up stroke

D D U D D U D D U D D U

BASIC "MARTILLO" BEAT

The entire beat is played on the small drum except 7 which is on the large drum. The large drum is on the right side.

1. LH thumb presses head
    RH fingers strike head near rim
2. LH fingers strike near center
3. RH fingers strike near center
4. LH thumb strikes near center
5. RH fingers strike near rim
6. LH fingers strike near center
7. RH fingers on rim of large drum
    for a "Pop" effect
8. LH thumb strikes and remains on head for first
    note of next measures.

BONGO DRUMS

R L R L R L R L

1 2 3 4 5 6 7 8

BASIC "TUMBAO" BEAT

1. Strike surface using a press stroke with left hand. (P = Press stroke)
2. Lift fingers with left thumb still pressing head strike head near rim with right hand, back portion of right palm strikes edge first allowing fingers to snap to head. (S = Slap Stroke)
3. Fingers strike head while hand is still pressing head. Release hand before right hand strikes next beat. (F = fingers)
4. Fingers of right hand strike surface of open head. (no left hand on head) (O = open drum sound)

CONGA DRUM

EXAMPLE 1

LH - P - Press stroke
LH - H - Heel of Palm
LH - F - Finger Tips
RH - S - Slap (Left hand remains on the head)
RH - O - Strike open head—let ring

H-F is similar to a heel-finger wave-like motion of the left hand.

EXAMPLE 2   **EXAMPLE 3**

Quinto — Highest pitched and smallest of conga drum family.

Conga — Standard sized drum.

Tumbadora — Lowest pitched conga with the largest diameter.

BASIC "BAQUETEO" BEAT

Left hand rests on low drum head stick across rim throughout.

1. Right stick strikes head
2. Right stick strikes rim shot
3. Left stick strikes rim — (hand remains on head)
4. Repeat #1
5. Repeat #2
6. Repeat #3
7. Right stick strikes high drum
8. Repeat #3

TIMBALES

The top line of the staff is for "paila", suspended cymbal or cowbell. "Paila" is the striking of the drum shells with timbale sticks; tip of the stick for soft and middle of the stick for loud playing. Fingers often strike the drum head instead of sticks for softer playing (see Cha Cha p. 12).

High Drum→ Low Drum

R R L R R L R L
1 2 3 4 5 6 7 8

INSTRUMENTS USED FOR
LATIN-AMERICAN
DANCES IN TWO

CHOCALLO*

By shaking the chocallo first eye-level (upward and away), then belt-level (downward and away), a slightly different tonal effect will be noticeable; the chocallo may be held horizontally at each end with both hands or in the center with one hand; shaking the tube in a vertical position produces a much softer sound.

AGOGO BELLS

Hold the bells in the left hand with the open end away from the player; touch the base of each bell if a muffled tone is desired.

MERENGUE-GUIRO
("Torpedo")

A guiro effect is obtained by scraping with a wire implement; a chocallo or shekere effect is produced by shaking the tube.

AFRICAN CLAVE
("Rosewood Claves")

Cupping the left hand directly beneath the hollowed clave opening will increase resonance when struck with the solid clave.

*Photos by Martin Cohen,
  Products by Latin Percussion, Inc.

CABASA

This round gourd is covered with a net of beads which may be slapped against the left palm for a staccato effect, shaken back and forth, like a chocallo for a rattling effect, or twisted while held in the left hand for a legato, scraping effect as the beads move against the chamber's outer wall.

AFUCHI-CABASA

This modern day cabasa which is made of a corrugated aluminum cylinder rotated against loosely slung metal beads, is capable of a louder scraping effect than the cabasa; playing techniques are similar.

VIBRASLAP

When the wooden ball is struck, metal rivets vibrate within a small hard wood chamber creating a long, buzzing rattle.

SHEKERE

Although the playing technique of this largest of gourd instruments is similar to the cabasa, the open end creates a deep resonant tone created when the palm of the hand strikes the closed end.

QUICAS

A medium-sized, single-headed drum suspended from the drummer's neck; fastened at the center of the head inside the shell is a wooden rod extending the length of the drum; holding a rosined cloth, the drummer rubs the rod, producing friction and a vocal-like sound while the left hand presses the head for pitch variance.

DANCES IN FOUR

RHUMBA

Fast Tempo   Iberia-Cuba

CLAVE

MARACAS

COWBELL

GUIRO

D   D U D   D U   D   D U D   D U

BONGOS (MARTILLO)

CONGA (TUMBAO)

TIMBALES (BAQUETEO)

DRUM SET

X = L.H. on snare drum
   with stick across rim.
   Left hand remains on head
   when right stick strikes snare head.

10

BOLERO RHUMBA

Slow

Cuba
Slower and softer
than the Rhumba

CLAVE

MARACAS

COWBELL (MUFFLED)

Optional

GUIRO (OPTIONAL)

D   U D   U D   U D   U

BONGOS

CONGA (TUMBAO)

R.H.   H F S F H O H O   H F S F H O H O

L.H.

TIMBALES

R.H.

L.H.
"Paila" on shells of both drums

DRUM SET

CHA CHA

Medium Slow   Cuba–U.S.

CLAVE

COWBELL (Mambo Cow Bell)

MARACAS

GUIRO

BONGOS (Martillo)

CONGA

TIMBALES

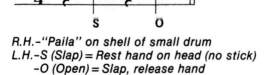

R.H.–"Paila" on shell of small drum
L.H.–S (Slap) = Rest hand on head (no stick)
*   –O (Open) = Slap, release hand*

DRUM SET

SLOW MAMBO

Slow four   **Cuba**

CLAVE

MARACAS

COWBELL

1.   2.   3.

GUIRO

D U D U *simile*

BONGOS (Martillo)

CONGA

R.H.   O H S   H F O O   H F S   H F O O

L.H.

TIMBALES   *"Paila" on shells of both drums*

1.
R.H.

L.H.

2. (Paila–R.H.)   3.
R.H.

L.H.   S   O   S   O

S = Slap
O = Open-release hand

DRUM SET

ide cymbal

13

PLENA

Fast four **Puerto Rico**

CLAVE

MARACAS

*PANDERETA or TAMBORIM

Hold this small drum in the hand so that the tips of the gripping fingers are able to press the head to alter the pitch.

X = Press head
O = Open sound
Strike the head with a short stick.

* *Slap small bongo drum for a suitable substitute*

CONGA

(Two drums-Both open sounds-Smaller drum on left.)

TIMBALES *(on open heads)*

DRUM SET

X = cross stick rim shot or open head

BEGUINE

Medium four   **Martinique**

CLAVE

MARACAS

BONGOS (Martillo)

CONGA

TIMBALES

(X = L.H. "cross" rim on low drum)

(R.H. "Paila" on shell of small drum)

DRUM SET

GUAJIRA

Medium slow four   Cuba

CLAVE

MARACAS

COWBELL *(optional)*

GUIRO *(optional)*

D   D U D   D U   D   D U D   D U

BONGOS
High Dr.

Low Dr.

Use Martillo fingering except on open head strike

CONGA
R.H.

L.H.

TIMBALES
R.H.

L.H.

S   O   S   O

R.H. "Paila"
L.H. on head–with hand (no stick)
S = Slap, rest hand on head
O = Open, slap and release hand

DRUM SET
Cup of
Ride cymbal

DANCES IN TWO
FAST MAMBO

In two   Cuba

CLAVE

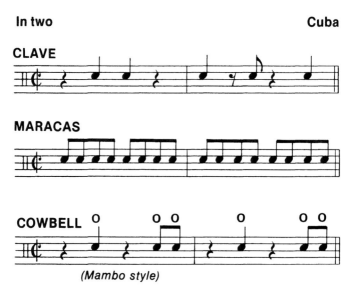

MARACAS

COWBELL

(Mambo style)

SECOND COWBELL *(optional)*

Alternate freely between open and closed end.

CONGA *(Quinto sized drum)*

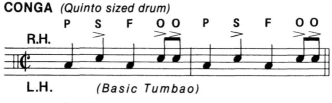

L.H.   *(Basic Tumbao)*

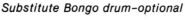

Substitute Bongo drum–optional

*CONGA *(Substitute Quica)*

TIMBALES

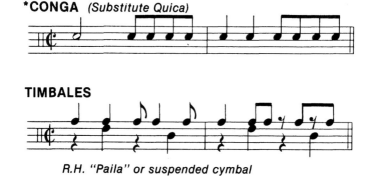

R.H. "Paila" or suspended cymbal
L.H. Sticks on open heads

DRUM SET

Ride cymbal

*Play basic Tumbao beat on Conga if no Quica

MERENGUE

In two-Moderately fast   **Dominican Republic**

CLAVE

*CHOCALLO

*Also called Tubo, Canza or Ganza.

COWBELL *(Muffled)*

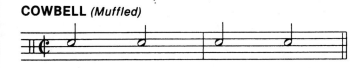

GUIRO (Merengue-type)

scrape D   D U D   D U   D   U D U D U

BONGOS *(Optional-Merengue Guiro more important if not covered)*

High Dr.

Low Dr.   *Open head sounds*

CONGA (Tumbadora if possible)

R.H.   O   S   O   S   O O O O

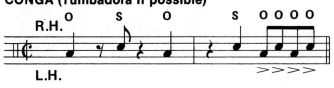

L.H.

TIMBALES (Tambora preferred)

R.H.

L.H. *(Sticks on open head)*

DRUM SET

SAMBA

In two-Moderately fast   **Brazil**

CHOCALLO

CABASA or AFUCHI

AGOGO BELLS

High Bell

Low Bell

MERENGUE GUIRO (Torpedo)

scrape D U D U D U D U   D U D U D U D U

CONGA

R.H. 1.

L.H.

R.H. 2.

L.H.

R.H. 3.

L.H.

TIMBALES

R   L R R   L R   R L R R   L

L.H. rests on large drum, strike stick across rim.
R.H. strikes large drum with left hand resting on head
  (third line).
R.H. strikes high drum, open head (fourth line).

DRUM SET

(Snares on or off)

〈 = *Left hand rests on head while pressing brush into head;
left hand remains on head when right stick strikes snare
head.*

19

BOMBA

In two–Medium Fast   Puerto Rico

CLAVE

SMALL COWBELL

STANDARD COWBELL

MERENGUE GUIRO (Torpedo)

QUINTO CONGA (Substitute Bongos)

CONGA

TUMBADORA (Low Conga)
or substitute low Timbale drum

DRUM SET

20

GUARACHA

In two-Medium   **Cuba**

CLAVE

Mambo Clave beat also suitable

MARACAS

COWBELL

BONGOS (Martillo)

CONGA

R.H.   H F S S H F O O   H F S S H F O O

L.H.

TIMBALES

R.H.

L.H.
  R.H.-"Paila"
  L.H.-Sticks on open heads

DRUM SET

21

BAION

In two—Moderately Fast   **Brazil**

CHOCALLO

CABASA or AFUCHI

MARACAS

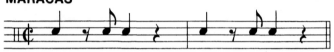

BONGOS

CONGA

TIMBALES

R.H. on open head—with open slap
L.H. rest hand on head for a closed slap

DRUM SET

X = L.H. rests on snare drum while pressing brush into head.

* BATUCATA
(See Glossary for instrument definitions)

In two–Moderately   **Brazil**

TAMBOURINE

RECO RECO

(or substitute Merengue Guiro [Torpedo])

QUICAS *(optional)*

(or ad-lib)

CABASA

Apito (Whistle) Ad-lib rhythms sparingly

BONGOS
(As substitute for Cachetas, strike small Bongo on head with stick)

TIMBALES *(As substitute for Tan-Tans)*

Strike low drum with stick

CONGA *(As substitute for Tambor-Surdos)*

DRUM SET

*The Batucata is not a dance but a full Brazilian rhythm section used for outdoor marching in street festivals. Drums are added when playing indoors.

*CALYPSO

In two　　　　　　　　　　　　　　　　　　　**West Indie**

CLAVE

MARACAS

BONGOS

(or play Martillo)

CONGA

TIMBALES

R.H. = "Paila"

One drum is often sufficient in this dance.
Bongos are preferred.

DRUM SET

*Usually background for a vocalist

AFRO-CUBAN DANCES
GUAGUANCO
(wa wan co)

In two-$\frac{6}{8}$ feel   Africa/Cuba

AFRICAN CLAVES

SHEKERÉ (or Torpedo substitute)

(shake Torpedo as large Chocallo)

TAMBORA (Bongo substitute) CASCARA

Cascara technique–strike the drum shell with sticks

QUINTO (Small Conga) *Solo ad-lib*

CONGA *(Medium size)*
Substitute Timbales, strike open heads with sticks

TUMBADORA (Large Conga)

DRUM SET

AFRO-CUBAN $\frac{6}{8}$

Bright two

Africa

MEDIUM PITCHED COWBELL

LOW PITCHED COWBELL

MARACAS

SHEKERÉ (Large Gourd or Torpedo)

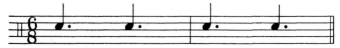

BONGOS

CONGA

P = Press stroke, leave hand on head for R.H. slap

TIMBALES

DRUM SET

SLOW AFRO-CUBAN

Slow four   **Africa**

AFRICAN CLAVE

MARACAS

COWBELL

GUIRO

BONGOS

CONGA

TIMBALES

R.H. "Paila"   L.H. Open heads

DRUM SET

CONGA

In Bright two   **Africa-Cuba**

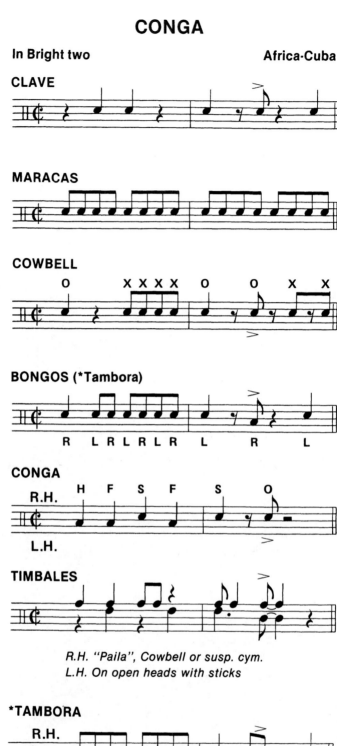

R.H. "Paila", Cowbell or susp. cym.
L.H. On open heads with sticks

*The Tambora is an excellent substitute for Bongos

AFRO DANCES
NAÑIGO

Bright two   Africa

"Paila" on shells of both drums

MASACOTE

Medium to Fast four   **Africa**

CLAVE

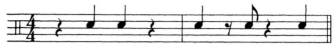

COWBELL

GUIRO

D   DUD   DU   D   DUD   DU

BONGOS (Martillo)

CONGA

Ad-lib generously

TIMBALES

R.H.–"Paila" (If no cowbell–play cowbell)
L.H.–Hands on head
P – Press stroke
O – Open snap

DRUM SET

Free ad-lib exchanges between drums are common

JAZZ STYLES
BOSSA NOVA

In four   **Brazil**

Since the introduction of the Bossa Nova in the six-
ties, as a jazz samba, the elements below are freely
utilized in the jazz, pop and rock idioms.

Element #1   CLAVE

Other instruments which might play this rhythm:
- **Temple Block**
- **Wood Block**
- **African Clave**
- **Cowbell** *(struck with soft mallet)*
- **One Agogo bell** *(lightly with small stick)*
- **One Bongo head** *(lightly with finger)*

Element #2   CHOCALLO

Other instruments which might play this rhythm:

Triangle (X = Damped   O = Open)

Tambourine (X = Shake   O = Slap)

Merengue Guiro, Reco-Reco or Guiro (with scraper),
Cabasa, Afuchi-Cabasa, Kameso, Maracas, Sand-
paper Block, Suspended Cymbal (with stick) or
Brushes scraping snare drum head.

Element #3   CONGA

Other suggested instruments:
Tan tan, Tambor-Surdo, Tumbadora

DRUM SET

(snares on)

FAST MAMBO—LATIN-JAZZ

Fast four

Cuba-U.S.

CLAVES

COWBELL

AFUCHI-CABASA

MARACAS

BONGOS (Martillo)

CONGA

L.H. (Basic Tumbao)

TIMBALES

R.H. Suspended cymbal
L.H. Sticks on open heads

DRUM SET

ride cymbal cup or cowbell

MONTUNO

Medium four   Cuba

CLAVES

MARACAS

COWBELL

GUIRO

D   D U D   D U   D   D U D   D U

BONGOS (Martillo)

CONGA

R.H.   H F S O P F S S   H F S O P F S S

L.H.

TIMBALES

R.H.

L.H.

R.H. "Paila"
L.H. Sticks on open head

DRUM SET

This is generally the section of a dance where the rhythm
instruments are featured. Rhythms in the melodic line are
developed within a short repeated phrase. Often the
rhythms accompany a soloist. Tempo or dynamics might
increase and rhythms could become more complex. Cuban
dances often feature a Montuno section.

NUEVA ONDA

Medium to fast three   **Venezuelan Indian/African**

Element #1   COWBELL

Other suggested instruments:
Temple Block, Wood Block, African Clave, Cowbell (struck with soft mallet), One Agogo Bell (lightly with small stick), One Bongo Head (lightly with finger).

Element #2   AFUCHI-CABASA

Other suggested instruments:
Chocallo, Triangle, Merengue Guiro, Reco-Reco or Guiro (with scraper), Cabasa, Kameso, Maracas, Sandpaper Block, Suspended cymbal (with sticks) or brushes scraping snare drum head.

Element #3   CONGA

Other suggested instruments:
Tan Tan, Tambor-Surdo, Tumbadora

DRUM SET

ROCK STYLES
ROCK STYLE CHA CHA

Slow tempo

COWBELL (Low pitched)

VIBRASLAP

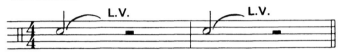

AFUCHI-CABASA

BONGOS

CONGA

TIMBALE

R.H. Suspended cymbal
L.H. Sticks on open heads

DRUM SET

snares on

SLOW ROCK (Latin)

Double-time feel is important

TRIANGLE

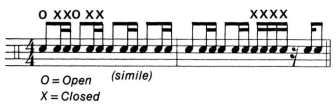

O = Open *(simile)*
X = Closed

VIBRASLAP

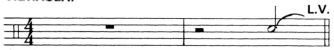

CHOCALLO

TAMBOURINE

CONGA

R.H.

L.H.

DRUM SET

closed Hi-Hat

(snares on)

36

MODERATE TEMPO ROCK (Latin)

CLAVES

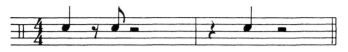

GUIRO

VIBRASLAP

TAMBOURINE or AFUCHI-CABASA

CONGA (Tumbao)

TIMBALES

R.H. Suspended cymbal
L.H. Sticks on open heads

DRUM SET

cowbell or ride cymbal

MODERATELY FAST ROCK (Latin)

CLAVE

CHOCALLO

COWBELL

BONGOS (Martillo)

CABASA

DRUM SET

(O = Open Hi-Hat)

(snares on)

FAST TEMPO ROCK (Latin)

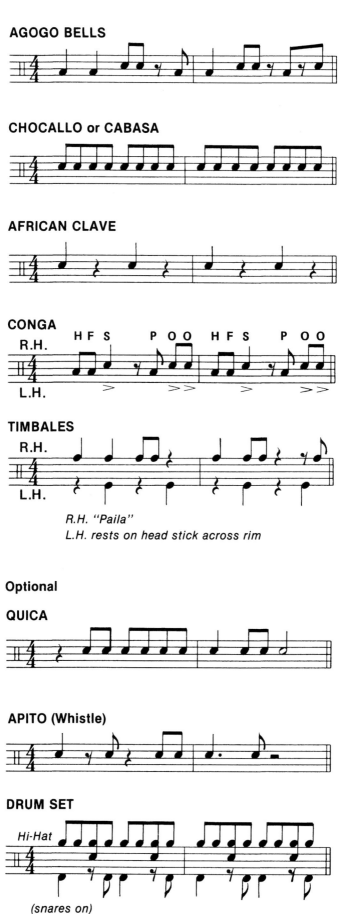

AGOGO BELLS

CHOCALLO or CABASA

AFRICAN CLAVE

CONGA

R.H.

H F S   P O O   H F S   P O O

L.H.

TIMBALES

R.H.

L.H.

R.H. "Paila"
L.H. rests on head stick across rim

Optional

QUICA

APITO (Whistle)

DRUM SET

Hi-Hat

(snares on)

REGGAE

Medium to fast tempo　　　　　　　　**Jamaica**

This rhythm introduced in the seventies freely utilizes varied instruments while employing the following basic rhythm elements.

Element #1

Element #1 could be played on:
Triangle, Cowbell, Chocallo, Tambourine, Paila (Timbale), Afuchi-Cabasa, Hi-Hat (closed).

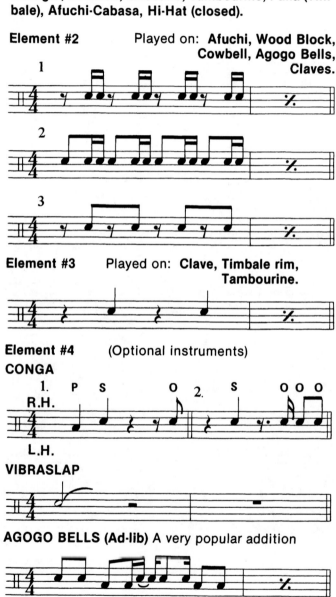

Element #2　　　　　Played on: **Afuchi, Wood Block, Cowbell, Agogo Bells, Claves.**

Element #3　　　Played on: **Clave, Timbale rim, Tambourine.**

Element #4　　　(Optional instruments)

CONGA

VIBRASLAP

AGOGO BELLS (Ad-lib) A very popular addition

DRUM SET
O = Open Hi-Hat

Develop your own instrumentation

REGGAE SHUFFLE

Varied tempos   Jamaica

Element #1

Suggested instrumentation:
Tambourine, Chocallo, Merengue Guiro (Torpedo), Afuchi-Cabasa.

Element #2

Suggested instrumentation:
Conga, Timbale (Low drum), Afuchi-Cabasa.

Element #3

Tambourine, Afuchi-Cabasa, Hi-Hat, Timbale rim.

Element #4

Bass drum (Drum set), Afuchi-Cabasa, Conga, Suspended cymbal (with stick).

Element #5   Fragments of the above

Guiro, Afuchi, Snare drum, Timbale rim.

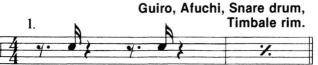

The third beat often includes an accessory

Cowbell, Clave, Wood Block

Explore combining both the suggested varied instrumentation and rhythms.

DRUM SET

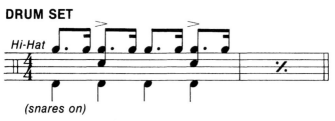

(snares on)

ARRANGER'S SUGGESTIONS

The Afro-Latin instruments have two main divisions which should be considered before scoring: accessory instruments which comprise the rhythm section and the drum family: bongos, conga and timbales.

Suggestions from the authentic dance forms could be expanded and varied from the rhythms in this book to fit the composition.

Arranging guidelines for the rhythm section:

1. *Select rhythmic elements from the melody and accompaniment of the composition.*

2. *Select rhythm instruments to best enhance the rhythmic character of the composition.* For example, a legato and subdued melody should be framed by a subtle and more legato sounding accessory, while a staccato and rhythmic melody should be enforced with a similar sounding rhythm section.

3. *Select instruments for their ability to blend and be compatable with the dance form.* A cowbell should be omitted if it does not blend. In Cuban dances a clave is essential. In Brazilian dances a chocallo or a shaking instrument is essential.

4. *Instruments should be selected for their dynamic intensity and playing characteristics.* The demands of an exciting jazz samba versus a quiet vocal ballad require two different sized chocallos to be used with different arm action.

5. *As a general rule, do not duplicate the same rhythmic element on more than one rhythm instrument.* Duplicating scraping instruments or shaking instruments tends to create a muddled background.

6. *Consider pitch and tone color carefully when combining instruments.* Multiple cowbells, congas or drums in general should have widely varied pitch differentiation for clear contrast. Special care should be exercised when combining metallic, wood, or gourd-like instruments. Similarity in tone might require a substitute or total elimination of one instrument.

AFRO-CUBAN DANCES

wood	striking	clave
gourd	shaking	maracas
metal	striking	cowbell
gourd	scraping	guiro
animal skins	striking	drums

Stronger African roots might produce multiple cowbells or multiple drums.

BRAZILIAN DANCES

metal tubos	shaking	chocallo
gourd	twist	cabasa or afuchi
metal	striking	agogo bells
tubos	scraping	reco reco
		(merengue guiro)
animal skins	striking	drums

Some dance rhythms are much more improvisational and innovative with a greater selection of instrumentation such as the Bossa Nova, Montuno, Batucata, Nueva Onda, suggested rock style Latin and Reggae.

ARRANGER'S SCORING EXAMPLES

Melody #1 (Moderate four)

The above melody seems to draw from a BOLERO RHUMBA rhythm and instrumentation (see Bolero Rhumba). The clave and maracas create the steady Rhumba rhythm; the guiro produces a legato scrape through beat one or two; cowbell has a strategic strike on open beat 3.

The drum family could add a more effective accompaniment if they used the Cha-Cha rhythm pattern (see Cha-Cha). Bongos would play straight eighth notes to match the melody; conga would be playing an open drum sound on the fourth beat which is left free in the melody; timbales also enforce the Rhumba rhythm with a less complex background.

Melody #2 (In two)

The rhythms contained in melody #2 suggest a Samba. Chocallo, afuchi-cabasa and timbales should remain as written under Samba (see Samba). The first Conga rhythm would fit the melody since it is less cluttered. I might omit the merengue-guiro since the rhythms are duplicated in the chocallo and would over emphasize the straight eighth feel. The agogo bells should be changed to better fit the melody:

ARRANGER'S SCORING EXAMPLES
continued

Melody #3 (In moderately slow four)

There are no strong rhythmic suggestions in the subdued legato style in melody #3. The background,
therefore, should not dominate rhythmically or
dynamically.

African clave and chocallo will play elements one
and two of a Bossa Nova beat respectively (see
Bossa Nova). The low pitched clave and legato style
small chocallo would be effective. Timbales will play
the beats under *Rock Style Cha Cha.* The suspended
cymbal will give a legato effect to the background
and the conga could play the beat under *Fast Tempo
Rock Latin* only at a slower pace. This conga beat
stresses the 2nd and 4th beats of the melody which
fits well with the open 2nd and 4th beats of the
melody. The purpose of this accompaniment is to
add an effective Latin flavor to the melodic content
without identifying with a specific dance form.

*Important: melodic content, rhythmic accompani-
ment* and *style of the music or dance form* determine
instrumentation and rhythms.

GLOSSARY

ABANICO *(ăh băh nē'koh)* A short drum fill on the small timbale utilizing rim shots and drum roll combinations.

AFRICAN CLAVE A large, hollow clave struck by a similar sized solid clave producing a dark wood click; not as penetrating as standard sized claves, but effective for subtle, low-pitched tone. (See pg. 8)

AFUCHI-CABASA *(ăh foo' chē-kăh băh' săh)* A modern day cabasa with similar playing techniques. (See pg. 9)

AGOGO BELLS *(ăh gō'gō)* Attached double bells shaped much longer than regular cowbells; tuned to an interval of approximately a third; produces a high pitched ring when struck with a stick. (See pg. 8)

APITO *(ăh pēē' tōh)* Whistle used in Brazilian festival street or marching bands; the leader uses the whistle as a rhythm instrument by blowing short blasts.

BAQUETEO *(băh kĕh tĕh' ōh)* The basic timbale beat utilized in Cuban style dances.

BATUCATA *(băh too kăh'dăh)* A complete Brazilian percussion section.

BONGOS *(bŏn' gō)* Usually made of wood shells, the two single-headed drums are attached and measure 6" and 8" in diameter; the soprano in the drum family, they are tuned to high pitches, penetrating large rhythm sections easily. (See pg. 5)

CABASA or CASABA *(kăh băh' săh or kăh săh' băh)* An authentic round gourd covered with a net of beads; used in Brazilian dance forms. (See pg. 9)

CACHETAS *(kăh schĭt' ĕh)* A tamborim-like drum only square shaped, not circular; it is struck with a small stick. (See the bongo part in the Batucata section, pg. 23)

CANZA *(kăhn' săh)* See Chocallo.

CASCARA *(kăhs kăh' răh)* Rhythm played on the shell of a tambora. (See Guaguanco, pg. 25)

CHARANGA *(chăh răn'găh)* A Cuban band featuring rhythm instruments, drums, violins and flutes.

CHOCALLO *(chŏh căh'yoh)* A long metal cylinder containing rice, sand, or seeds; it is shaken and the filler strikes the walls of the tube; a very popular instrument in Brazilian dance forms; also called tubo, canza or ganza. (See pg. 8)

CINQUILLO *(sēn kēē'yōh)* This important five note rhythm played by the claves is the foundation for Latin-American rhythms; all other instruments are guided by the "Cinquillo" rhythm.

CLAVE *(klăv′ěhs)* Two medium-sized 8 inch long pieces of resonant wood approximately one inch in diameter struck together for a cutting "wood click" effect. (See pg. 4)

CONGA *(kŏn′gäh)* Made of wood or fiberglass, the longest sized drum in the Afro-Latin drum family; average size 11" in diameter and 28" deep with a single muleskin or goatskin head; the conga is the bass voice and very resonant. (See pg. 6)

COWBELL Actually a cow's bell without the bell clapper; hand held, struck with a wood stick or clave, with the open end facing toward the audience; an important time keeper in the Afro-Latin rhythm section. (See pg. 4)

GANZA *(găhn′săh)* See Chocallo.

GUIRO *(gōō ēē′rōh)* Made of a gourd and scraped with a stick; the corrugated type notched surface is brushed lightly with a small stick, creating a smooth, percussive scrape-like effect; metal scrapers on animal horns are also utilized. (See pg. 4)

KAMESO *(căh měh′sōh)* A shaking tube similar to the chocallo except the construction is of wood or gourd instead of metal; this effect is softer and lower in pitch.

MARACAS *(măh răh′ kăhs)* Hollowed gourds with an attached handle; dried seeds are placed inside and sharp wrist motions cause the seeds to rattle against the walls of the gourd; shell size and seed size determine pitch of the instrument. (See pg. 4)

MARTILLO *(măr tē′yōh)* Basic bongo beat.

MERENGUE-GUIRO *(měh rěhn′ gā - gōō ēē′ roh)* A large, torpedo shaped cylinder with shot inside and a corrugated exterior outside; also called "torpedo". (See pg. 8)

PAILA (PAIL) *(păh e′ăh)* Striking the timbale shells with sticks for a "pail" tone effect.

PANDEIRO *(păh děh e′rōh)* A tambourine.

PANDERETA *(păhn děh rěh′ tăh)* A small, Puerto Rican drum similar to tamborim used in the Plena (see tamborim).

QUICA *(kēēk′ ăh)* Medium-sized, single-headed drum suspended from the neck of the drummer; produces a vocal-like sound. (See pg. 9)

QUIJADA *(kē hăh′ dăh)* Jawbone of an ass with loose teeth that rattle when struck with the fist (see vibraslap).

QUINTO *(kēn′ tōh)* Smallest of the conga drum family.

RECO-RECO *(rěk′ ōh - rěk′ ōh)* Hollow bamboo cylinder with ridges carved on the outside; a small bamboo stick held in the right hand is scraped against the outer wall for a guiro-like effect.

SHEKERE *(shĕh' kĕh rĕh)* A large gourd with an open end; larger than the cabasa and strung with beads. (See pg. 9)

TAMBORA *(tăm bōhr' ăh)* A double-headed drum suspended horizontally from the neck of the drummer; a stick strikes the right head, while the fingers of the left hand strike the left head.

TAMBOR-SURDO *(tăhm bōhr'- sōor'dōh)*
Barrel-shaped, double-headed Brazilian drum struck with a mallet; the left hand is used to damp the head; the lowest tone of the Brazilian drum family is played first with a short, damped tone followed by a second broad and dark ring. (See conga in the Batucata section, page 7.)

TAMBORIM *(tăhm bōhr'ĕm)* A small drum resembling a tambourine without jingles; the single head is struck with a small stick; left hand finger pressure against the head alters the pitch.

TAMBOURINE *(tăm bōō rĕn')* A 10'' round shallow hoop with a single head and jingles (metal disks) inserted in the frame; the head is often removed; shaken for a shuffle effect or struck for accents.

TAN-TAN *(tăhn-tăhn)* A shallow, double-headed drum in the Brazilian drum family; rhythm is articulated with the fingers of the hands; first a long tone (RH) followed by a short, slapping blow (LH). (See timbale part in Batucata section, pg. 23.)

TIMBALES *(tēm băh' lĕhs)* 11'' and 14'' single-headed, metal-shelled drums mounted on a floor stand; the drums are usually tuned to an interval of a fourth and the goat skin heads are struck with thin 3/8'' dowelled sticks. (See pg. 7)

TORPEDO See merengue-guiro.

TRIANGLE A metal triangle held in the hand; struck with a heavy metal beater on the two sides not held by the hand; gripping fingers open and close to produce open and closed tonal effects.

TUBO *(tōō' bōh)* See chocallo.

TUMBADORA *(tōōm băh dōr' ăh)* Largest of the conga drum family.

TUMBAO *(tōōm băh' ōh)* Basic conga drum beat.

VIBRASLAP A metal rod with a wood ball at one end and a hard wood chamber containing rivets at the other end; manufactured to imitate the quijada effect. (See pg. 9)